SUSTu

T0101882

The Mountain / West Poetry Series
Stephanie G'Schwind, Donald Revell, Kazim Ali,
Dan Beachy-Quick & Camille T. Dungy, series editors

We Are Starved, by Joshua Kryah
The City She Was, by Carmen Giménez Smith
Upper Level Disturbances, by Kevin Goodan
The Two Standards, by Heather Winterer
Blue Heron, by Elizabeth Robinson
Hungry Moon, by Henrietta Goodman
The Logan Notebooks, by Rebecca Lindenberg
Songs, by Derek Henderson
The Verging Cities, by Natalie Scenters-Zapico
A Lamp Brighter than Foxfire, by Andrew S. Nicholson
House of Sugar, House of Stone, by Emily Pérez
&Luckier, by Christopher J Johnson
Escape Velocity, by Bonnie Arning
We Remain Traditional, by Sylvia Chan
The Lapidary's Nosegay, by Lara Candland
Furthest Ecology, by Adam Fagin
The Minuses, by Jami Macarty
Dears, Beloveds, by Kevin Phan
West : Fire : Archive, by Iris Jamahl Dunkle
Daughters of Harriet, by Cynthia Parker-Ohene
Susto, by Tommy Archuleta

SUSTO

TOMMY ARCHULETA

POEMS

The Center for Literary Publishing
Colorado State University

Copyright © 2023 by Tommy Archuleta.
All rights reserved.

For information about permission to reproduce
selections from this book, write to:
The Center for Literary Publishing
attn: Permissions
9105 Campus Delivery
Colorado State University
Fort Collins, Colorado 80523-9105.

Printed in the United States of America.

Library of Congress Cataloging-in-Publication Data

Names: Archuleta, Tommy, 1965- author.
Title: Susto : poems / Tommy Archuleta.
Other titles: Mountain west poetry series.
Description: Fort Collins, Colorado : The Center for Literary Publishing,
Colorado State University, [2023] | Series: The mountain/west poetry series
Identifiers: LCCN 2022052304 (print) | LCCN 2022052305 (ebook) | ISBN
9781885635853 (paperback) | ISBN 9781885635860 (ebook)
Subjects: LCSH: Shamans--Poetry. | Healing--Poetry. | LCGFT: Poetry.
Classification: LCC PS3601.R3896 S87 2023 (print) | LCC PS3601.R3896
(ebook) | DDC 811/.6--dc23/eng/20221125
LC record available at https://lccn.loc.gov/2022052304
LC ebook record available at https://lccn.loc.gov/2022052305

The paper used in this book meets the minimum requirements of the
American National Standard for Information Sciences-Permanence of Paper for Printed
Library Materials, ANSI Z39.48-1984.

Publication of this book was made possible by a grant
from the National Endowment for the Arts.

**National
Endowment
for the Arts**
arts.gov

ART WORKS.

For Pop, Nan, and my curandera and mother,
Mary F. Archuleta (1927–2013).

sus • to: *n.m.* 1. shock. 2. magical fright.
—— as defined by Eliseo "Cheo" Torres
in *Healing with Herbs and Rituals*

CONTENTS

I

3   Again the first lamb

4   Look at your hands

5   What calm

6   Three hawks at the entrance

7   Bless the hands

8   Climb until the trees begin to thin

9   Tracks

10   One tree alive still for every three

11   If a higher one then a lower

12   Never burn

13   *Remedio: San Antonio de Padua*

14   First one then three

15   Rose petals

16   It was you the other day

17   You like not knowing

II

21   The blue jays and blackbirds

22   Another velvet painting please

23   A stone a leaf a stash of cranes

24   I never told you this but in one

25   All those faces

26   Love as seed or love as plow

27   *Remedio: Añil del Muerto*

28   I forget

29   From here these clouds must

30   From dust this hope

31   There

32   Most nights

33   *Remedio: Preparación*

34   Whatever you say here

III

37   This place
38   Say little knives
39   Her welcoming the first frost
40   To survive this side
41   Anymore I wake
42   My last days
43   You know the house
44   *Remedio: Mimbre*
45   Now with every *Yes*
46   Tell me again about
47   Tiny screams and wingbeats
48   When you get like this
49   Yell all you want
50   María Santísima
51   *Remedio: Yerba de Víbora*

IV

55   *Remedio: La Llamada*
56   What if hell isn't a world
57   Please Lord
58   Mother blue
59   Vision after vision
60   What of the shrine to Jacob
61   My poor mirror
62   No humming flying out of
63   Another long night
64   Just like you said
65   He wrote the words *Love*

V

69   I keep asking but nothing comes back

70   I swear

71   I never know if it's dawn

72   *Remedio: Recuperación*

73   Finally

74   Sweetbread

75   The hard candy yes

76   What if instead of praying

77   Black pearls

78   *Remedio: Ocotillo*

79   Same as you

80   Dear Ruin

81   There go the trees stirring

83   *Afterword*

84   *Acknowledgements*

I

Again the first lamb
I led to slaughter
                    and again the same

three angels
mending each other's wings
at the river's edge

Maybe they know the whereabouts
of the starling that flew
out of Mother's mouth

Look at your hands
she kept saying

Take them to the light
Bathe them in it

Study them
good and up close then drive

them down past the snow
to the red loam

and watch what
happens next

What calm
in the way the gravedigger

unbuttons his coat
and the frozen

ground below him
How it longs to be opened

You learn not to wave
at the soldier

coatless always
wandering the roads and fields

He's home now
for good

says his mother
Yes   home now

for good
say the wolves

Three hawks at the entrance
where for centuries
nine stood watch

You worry too much about
the moth you lost
to all those o's

and 8s she carved around
your lantern

Maybe all the sobbing
isn't sobbing
Maybe it's humming

Humming out to lace this
fever and me
together for good

Bless the hands
in the mirror whoever they

belong to the brown recluse
somewhere

in my room
and all those children gunned down

in that school and
the little boy ghost too

who lives up on the roof   god
how I envy

his nerve
His patience

His boots
His view of the river

Climb until the trees begin to thin
but don't spit

out the tiny white
stones your mother gave you

Not until we reach
what's left of the gates

It's getting harder and harder
to breathe isn't it
                    But don't blame
him for not being
the father you wanted

Instead help me name
the little bird

soon to fly out
of your stigmata

You go first

Tracks
and more tracks   same as those

leading from the well
to the house

Didn't they find a man not
far from here

His eyes not gone
as in closed forever but gone

as in someone or something
had carved

both of them
clean out   I don't know

Maybe one of us
had better cut pine branches

weave his memory a cross
while the other tends

to the fire
through the coming frost

One tree alive still for every three
downed by lightning

five by disease
Bad leg or not whoever's

following us stopped here
for the night

but never slept
Never ate a single thing

We'll sleep with osha in
our boots tonight

to keep the snakes
away but if the ancients come

for our souls nothing will stop
them our bodies

left for the cold
and wolves to fight over

If a higher one then a lower
one too must exist

That's what the choke
cherry tree

kept saying
the last night I slept under her

That and something about
the relics of

Saint Cecilia
shifting a bit when kissing

the lid of her
glass casket

Never burn
unsent hate letters to the drought

unless you want for
your people

forty more
years under the god-given

blades that took
your great

grandfather's
fields and never whatever you do

curse the fever that took
your beloved

mother
Doing so will only

wake then
maim the darkest thing

inside you
Believe you me

Remedio: San Antonio de Padua

For lost objects and lost money, go without. For loss of vigor for life, begin the rite at once by setting down on paper the patient's full name and date of birth. Second, obtain a small statue of the saint. Wrap all contents in cloth, secure with string, and toss the bundle into the river. Look for winged signs over the coming days when awake and when dreaming. They will appear if your offering stays intact for nine full days.

First one then three
then five
            now seven
each child bound to her own tree
mouth to foot

the rope spun on looms
built nowhere near here

Same for the captain's silk scarf
white as the white
of the children's eyes

his face just
like the river's
            at night   covered
with cuts deep
enough to see through

Rose petals
Some red some white   one
black as the lake's face

at night come summer
and wingless as my moth

I say we name you all Dolores
after the time something
dark in Mother
                    Something smelling
like smoke and wetdog
wanted to drown me

Dolor

Spanish for pain
god and   sometimes   fever

It was you the other day
wasn't it

Not the you
when you were real

little but the you unable
to breathe

flying in and
out of me without my knowing

the two of us ending
up in the pine

crowns somehow
floating

there à la
Teresa de Ávila

You like not knowing
how you got here
            don't you and how light
blue light keeps flying

out of my eyes
and mouth whenever
the music decides

to stop

Not everyone
has the nerve to keep going

Not even the bravest
gone for good

bloodmother
watching over what's left
of her only son

II

The blue jays and blackbirds
How loud they sang

that night cold
as it was and so far upriver

I see round lights too sometimes
dancing in the field

no dog will cross
Still smell snakeroot burning

Or is that hair
Maybe I'm sleeping still

Maybe you're not
Maybe I'm someone

else's son praying
they soon find me

Another velvet painting please
of the mother

of God please
God to replace the one

my horse ate
Or are we given one and one only

every time around
One scythe-like moon under her

One gold brooch forged
into a cross

One starstrewn
bluegreen gown eaten here

and there by cloud-white
moths   what else

A stone a leaf a stash of cranes
bathing ungodly late

where the river
slows most

Soon you will know
every window back home
once nailed shut now

opens and closes freely
That every saint you snapped
in two now stands

whole on the sills
and dressers of every room

waiting there for you
the wolf you

the crow you
the weary supplicant

I never told you this but in one
dream I'm watching

me burn
the robe she died in

In another it's some man
with no arms

(maybe
no face) singing *Here I am Lord*

He's naked and standing
in a field

years fallow
the song's shifting wiry

shadow eating half
dead funeral

flowers in
the arroyo nearby

All those faces
in the floor

The tiny chunks of coal
I keep finding

in my bed
in my boots

in my mouth

and no matter how high
or far he threw all twenty-six letters
he loved to cut up

they would spell *Forgive me*
every time when
they landed

and wherever
they would land
he would swear never again to snap

the hand of Mary clean off
just to see what
color her blood is

Love as seed or love as plow
End as end
or end as opening

Either way   why go
on fearing
the dark part

god part doorway
Go ahead

Ask me

Remedio: Añil del Muerto

To aid safe passage, pick the blue-green leaves when the flowers have fully bloomed. Air for one day and one night prior to mashing. Coat the tip of a wooden stake with the pulp before driving it into the foot of the loved one's grave. Bury the rest of the pulp at the base of the headstone. Pray ceaselessly as before.

I forget   was it you or me
they caught

welcoming
the first frost with drums

and bellflowers the year Mother's
mind went the

way of the orchard
You or me

who hears laughter   ribbons
of it coming

from the grave
with not one single deathgreen

plastic vase to speak of
What torture

of all tortures
wouldn't you say for

the one sunstruck
plastic flower

From here these clouds must
look black to him
Black as his first guitar

Ever notice how hard
it is to breathe (when you can't stop

bleeding)   here
where every little hook you find
makes a little cut that hates

the word *heal*   here
where time means smoke end
means flying and the eyes

The eyes this close to useless

From dust this hope
to dye red

rounds
and rounds of bread gold

as the sun   (imagine) and
on the bridge

railing the crow
behind me saying the higher

you fly the darker life
becomes

the darker
life becomes the more you

find forms
of silence

you never
before knew existed

There
The mayors plow horse

can now roam free
At least until noon when the hunters

return from the canyon
the scrub jays

leave the fields
for the river

the dying review
yesterday's vespers and Father

sits down to write his
daily love

letter to suffering
With or without pen and paper

You're right
I best go check on him

Most nights
it's the cane carved from redwood

you come to first followed by
the spool of chain

near the buckboard wagon
Then comes the free

standing door
that when opened and walked

through takes you to the towering
black iron oven

its mouth seldom
open except to eat more apple

tree branches that scream
to use your

words just
like the Pueblo children

Remedio: Preparación

When preparing to call the soul back, first ask the Earth for permission to take from her only what will be needed. Next, offer a New Fire prior to gathering osha root, mugwort, and rosemary. Bathe the entire catch in river water. Soak overnight. The next day, mash then combine all contents in a glass container. A mason jar will do, but do not cover. Add rubbing alcohol to the mixture to release all healing properties. Place the jar in a dry, dark place for three days and three nights.

Whatever you say here
dies twice the instant you say it

Or haven't you noticed

No different than
the snapdragons
                    we threw down
into the dampdark
of Mother's open grave
But don't feel bad   I never know

who's talking either
Me   you   or the furthest star
whose light though brave

will neverever reach us

III

This place

The light here

These clouds

(if that's what they are)

Everything really   red as the earth as you enter
        the valley from the south

My poor hands

Just look at them

This one a day maybe two away from ether

But this one   this one   thankgod is still able
        somehow to open

and close

Open and close

Say little knives
litter the ground of every life

we survive
Now say the mind stores

some but the body
houses all

Only say these things
over and over

crawling end
to end across the valley floor

and I'll tell you what your
true name

and symbols
mean in Spanish

Her welcoming the first frost
mid-orchard at dawn
with song   the surest way to offend
    the god of ruin

Her and a basket of bellflowers
naming them one
by one in the cool cellardark

Her picking apricots in a corner
of the living room
in the middle

of the night enrobed
in moonlight enough to mum you

Pictures you never took
but that live
like she does inside of you

To survive this side
This side

where love
keeps rhyming everything

with loss   are there
any maps

to a far
less crushing sorrow

Aka
breathing

No
But if you keep singing to me

till your tongue whitens
your throat clenches

                    ‹ tires   raws

I'll let you steal
more apples

Anymore I wake
as if holding a sword

My handbones unwilling to unfold

Just like my father's
And every other father before him

No more food left
No water

Nothing but the moon
and darkest
stars to live on

Nothing to come quell
the loneliness
rivaling

that of the
frozen canyon floor

My last days
May they pass

slow as blacksmoke
begins the

new prayer
father wrote

just yesterday   I
forget

how the
rest goes

No
No that one he stole

from Adam
I'm sure

who wrote it
the first night he spent

alone just outside
the Garden

You know the house
nearest the field where nothing grows

You know the markings
over the doorway

the stick of milkweed
smoldering always near the hole

in the dirt living
room floor

and in the bedroom
you know too the altar to St. Raphael

the darkest angel
of all   yes

You know well
all these things and yet still you go

Remedio: Mimbre

When contacting those gone to the afterlife, pick the blossoms at their whitest. Wash with holy water and air-dry. Save to paper what needs saying. Christen the note with fire at dusk. Collect the ashes in glass and cover with white cloth. Come nightfall combine all and crush down to a fine powder. Next, bundle the mixture in white cloth, tie with fishing line, and place the message at the base of the traveler's headstone.

Now with every *Yes*
comes a flying
                    glass casket
high up in the
blessed afterdark

Nothing inside her locket

Nothing inside the tiny
cedar box under
her side of the bed   Now then

would it kill you to say
the word *empty*

What if I told you doing
so would help you forget
not only your body

but your tongue too
Go on   answer me

Tell me again about
the saint they named me after

About how she floated
when she prayed

and how you can't be
alive and a saint at the same time

You just can't

You have to be dead first

Tiny screams and wingbeats
almost always now only

much louder when I do this

Don't tell me it's the moth
whose wings we tore off

after what happened
happened for the last time in

the coatroom on the last day
    of catechism

When you get like this
it reminds me

of the time
she poured holy water down

the wellshaft and burned
lavender sprigs

at sundown
Who knows what tongue

she sang in that day
Or why since then I start to sing

whenever this close to
the dying

Singing as
if I've always known

that hearing is the last
sense to go

Yell all you want
It doesn't help
                does it
Neither does sitting up
Or jumping

out of bed   Why
Because the quiet
won't let you
                the nights
now lasting twice
as long as Father's

That's why

María Santísima   believe me
I've kissed

every baby
Jesus in this house

Doused myself with citron and
dandelion smoke

Swept clean every sill and threshold
with pine branches

cut from the gorge
Cut no matter how loud

and backwards
the voices got   Now what

Remedio: Yerba de Víbora

For unwelcomed visions and voices, make an amulet from the herb's freshly cut flowers, a chain from the stronger stems. One worn for nine full days while fasting. A poultice will suffice for seasons other than fall. Be sure to christen the patient's hands and feet before treatment, never after. Should the unwanted events persist, summon the services of a good priestess without too much delay.

IV

Remedio: La Llamada

Two clean, white bedsheets will be needed. Smudge all windowpanes in the house with copal. Next, have the patient lie down on the bed faceup after bathing. Place the first sheet over the body, leaving only the hands, feet, and head exposed. Spread the second sheet under the bed, tying each corner to each leg of the bed. Be sure to crack open the bedroom window an inch or two. Begin now to sweep the body with a wand of copal, mint leaves, and lavender. Repeat the patient's full name over the coming hours, adding, "I now call your spirit back to your body." Stop only to pray, rest, drink water.

What if hell isn't a world
of fire or ice but
one with no one to tell

anything to   like the moon's
hands are full
always with slowing or

Father is dying but I promise
not to bury him

before he does
Or light is light no matter how
dark things get

Or how the Little Flower
everyone's favorite candlesaint

loves to rhyme coughing with
coffin now
in French

Now in Spanish
Now in the sun's own
mother tongue

Please Lord tell the boy wherever he is that I fixed all the windows and doors in the house and all the saints he broke in half I fixed those too only you know why my hands won't open the way they used to and why most days forgive me I can't stand the sight of food

Mother blue   mother root

Mother ever patient   is it
true what they say
                that you took
my body from this world

the one of trees
and light and
swallowed me down

blood bones
boots and all

Of all she took
with her why not too

the stand of elms where
the river slows

most and only strangers go
drawn there

by what sounds
to them

at first
like laughter

Vision after vision

You mean earth darksoft as blood don't   you

Earth meaning wave after wave

Which one's the wave and which one's falling

Falling on all fours

Or singing

Maybe singing is what you mean

Singing out to guide

Yes guide more than comfort one
the whole way down

What of the shrine to Jacob
Joseph's father

What about the bowl
for offerings

only the dead
see the speaking stones arranged

around it and the nameless
roadside crosses

from here
to the ghost of the orchard

And what of your own
ashes Father

Who left will
collect and bury them

if I go before
you do

My poor mirror   blacked
out for good

looks like (if you lie a lot or even
sometimes and

love to burn
things not wood you can have

bad dreams forever
can't you)

It's OK to not know
where you are
                even if you're
inside someone
else's bedtime prayer   even

your own mother's
when she was little

It's OK too to keep
rhyming blood
              with love
until they find you

If they ever do

No humming flying out of
the hangman's
great great granddaughter

Maybe her son took it
with him the instant
                    friendly fire
took him   and why not

Grandmother took the sound
of cranes bathing ungodly
late where the river once ran clearest

Mother took the faint taps
of rose petals landing
face-first on the kitchen floor

Who knows what sound you'll get
        to take

But you best choose one soon
or one will be chosen for you

Another long night
Another visit

Only this time
she was floating the way

her first doll would
whenever

they locked
it up sand pouring out

one hand a morning glory
in the other and

Nothing but nothing
spins faster than the sun

coming from
somewhere inside of her

Only this time the whole
world was

on fire
Not just me and

my horse
and the moon

Just like you said   someone
not me dyed

my wings redred
as the words

Jesus says here
and there in my motel Bible   and

I touched the dark long
enough to fall

in love
with the way it touches

me back
just like you said

He wrote the words *Love*
christened by sorrow only to cut

each letter up and bury them
Loons two of them sang in unison

Something shifted behind him
Something he never

saw never made out
In time a lost stranger would

bed down near there
Build a fire

Dream of finding breadcrumbs
A mapmaker some

said he was
One seldom able to sleep

Let alone rid his mind of the
graves he had robbed

V

I keep asking but nothing comes back

when *Please forgive me*
comes flying out of my mouth

Is it because everything you do
is written down before you do it

My love for the smell of wetdog
for instance and that I once
no twice stole Father's bonewhite

pocketknife and who really took
the picture of me naked
in the mayor's beanfield

and who exactly found Mother's
musty wedding gown
and wore it for three whole days

after they gave her
tiny body back to the earth

That day by far the darkest and longest of all

I swear   floaters everywhere
up and down the gorge
My boots wetwet

My horse who
knows where   hopefully home
waiting for the moon to show

But still nothing as to how
my wings got so blued
and broken

So many others here too
Most you can feel
Most you can

Wait   it must be noon
The hour Father stops hoping
they find me

and starts praying
for twice more suffering

I never know if it's dawn

or dusk when root hunting this far down

the canyon's mouth

Or which world I'll end up

entering when surfacing

The one mothered by fire   the one

of numbers posing as letters

or the one whose ground

is made of clouds voices

and parts of dark short songs

that are really one long dark song each

and every note nowhere near holy

Remedio: Recuperación

Build a White Fire in thanks once the spirit has returned. Give
the patient hot tea to drink, composed of chamomile, linden,
and passion flowers. Present the eldest member of the family
with red cedar shavings to be burned at noon the following
day. Make a small bundle of all remaining herbs used for the
recapture. Instruct the patient to carry the bundle for six days
and nights. On the morning of the seventh day, join the patient
in burying the bundle in the family field or garden.

Finally   the apple Mother stole from Eve

How many plagues and winters
have you seen

How many wars
have come and gone with no victor

for you to grieve
and how many fires christened

alms burned
vows written only to be sung halfheartedly
        come Christmas

Please then   mouth *harvest* with me

Sweetbread   yes Father
I made some

But only
enough for you me and the ghosts

inside us both
None for the wolves and none

for the crows either
Mijo

forgive our forefathers for what
they did to

the children
of the trees

I forgive you for taking all
that you took

from me
Now forgive yourself for all

that you've taken from
the earth

I will Father   I will
But we need

to change
and feed you first

The hard candy yes

The guess which hand
not so much
                but the cold
the cold I remember

That and the bad having
my heart all to itself winter
in   winter out

None of us is ever fully alone
are we   never
too far from being

touched by the forever cold
or those alive still
only barely

Think of the star
you'll see tonight who died

a zillion light-years ago
and whose deathlight

we barely
see flickering

What if instead of praying
for a happy death

we pray to death
herself and ask her nicely to heal

our wings   Or better yet we'll
make sure we look

at our hands real good
tonight when dreaming

cut and bloodied as they are
from all that clinging that way we

can fly the dream wherever
we want to go

Like to where
Mom is or where or where

our horse went to
Or maybe even to Mexico

Black pearls
black pearls

black pearls each
sings Father

from sleep
and through each a hole

bored for the lengthening
chain of days

to pass through
Not even goat's milk

nor sweetbread will he eat
and only Job

in from tending
his own fields

will he rise
to greet

To weep
with and speak to

Remedio: Ocotillo

To forgive one's beloved for dying, pick the long, feather-like, crimson flowers in early spring, when the desert is in bloom. Boil in river water only. Let cool. Drink at once. Drink when waking, at noon, and at bedtime each day for three full weeks thereafter. If resentment persists, go to your beloved's grave daily and pray for forgiveness until sound sleep and appetite return.

Same as you

I hear the voice cellardark
in places with talk

of bonewhite lilies
and blind forgiveness

The fever   it's in us
for good isn't it Father

Just like the valley
Just like the moon

and the rabbit I
whipped pillowcased and

buried believing
that much in

resurrection
same as you Father

Same as you

Dear Ruin
I'm sorry

but nothing will call Father
away from

his window
Offer him food or drink

and he closes his eyes
Offer your

hand to him
or place yours over his and

he'll just talk and talk
about the light

and the way it
breaks as who we truly

are leaves
the body

further
and further

behind
xoxoxo

There go the trees stirring
storm-like

again
Last time it was

the whirrs
of being held underwater   one

hand sewing
closed who

knows whose eyes
the other

signing
the word   *womb*

over
and over

AFTERWORD

In the wake of my mother's death, in that sheer-white numbness, Pop and I found among her things a homemade book on *curanderismo*. Its contents pair physical, mental, and spiritual ailments with a particular herb, plant, or root native to northern New Mexico. The instructions on how to prepare and administer each treatment (*remedio*) run from precise to vague. The paper stock is not of this century, nor of the last; its margins are filled with notes in Spanish and English, some in pencil, some in pen. And while the writing style of the notes varies greatly, here and there Mother's longhand stands out. Soon after this discovery, another came my way in the form of a line that continues to play to this day: *To love deeply is to grieve deeply.* Along the ground of this line a sinkhole appeared, and down I went, emerging years later with something close to the book you now hold in your hands, kind reader.

ACKNOWLEDGEMENTS

Thank you to the editors of the following journals in which earlier and present versions of the poems in this work have appeared:

The Academy of American Poets Poem-a-Day: "*Remedio: Ocotillo*" and "My last days"

Guesthouse: "I never told you this but in one" (as "In One"), "Rose petals" (as "What if I stay like this"), "All those faces," "Her welcoming the first frost" (as "You leaving the orchard"), and "*Remedio: Yerba de Vibora*"

Snapdragon: "*Remedio: Añil del Muerto*" and "I never told you"

New England Review: "*Remedio: San Antonio de Padua*" (as "San Antonio de Padua"), "Vision after vision," "Same as you," "Another velvet painting please" (as "Another velvet mother"), "*Remedio: Mimbre,*" "Dear Ruin," and "There go the trees stirring" (as "There go the trees")

House Mountain Review: "*Remedio: Recuperación,*" "Tell me again," "Tiny screams," and "The time she poured holy"

Lily Poetry Review: "Again the first lamb," "Look at your hands," "What calm," and "Three hawks"

2022 New Mexico Poetry Anthology: "*Remedio: La Llamada*"

This work might never have seen daylight if not for the undying generosity and loving support of my dear friend and mentor Dana Levin; the astounding eyes, ears, and mind of Jane Huffman; the deft writerly guidance and friendship of Michael Mercurio; and the quiet wisdom and inspiration I received from Christopher Johnson that fed draft after draft of this work over the years.

Honorable thanks to Valerie Martínez, Greg Glazner, and Matt Donovan for making those four extremely short years at College of Santa Fe (RIP), the unforgettable and cathartic experience it was for me and my family. Honorable thanks also to poet, writer, and devoted educator Lisa Chavéz, whose poetry workshops in the MFA program at the University of New Mexico provided fertile ground from which the seeds of *Susto* first took root.

Undying thanks to The Center of Literary Publishing at Colorado State University for adding this work to the Mountain/West Poetry Series catalog. Undying thanks also to the series editors, especially Kazim Ali, for tirelessly championing it, and Stephanie G'Schwind, for the wealth of warm guidance and support in shaping and bringing this collection to light. And most certainly, gobs of warm thanks to the entire production team that is Laura Roth, Bianca Melendrez Valenzuela, C. E. Janecek, and Carolina Bucheli-Peñafiel.

Special thanks to Erin Long for *Susto's* cover art.

Lastly, I wish to thank a thousand times Eliseo "Cheo" Torres, the gifted educator of curanderismo at the University of New Mexico—and a curandero himself—who tirelessly guided my research journey into this ancient medicinal art form.

This book is set in Perpetua and Letter Gothic
by The Center for Literary Publishing
at Colorado State University.

Copyediting by Laura Roth.
Proofreading by Bianca Melendrez Valenzuela.
Book design and typesetting by C. E. Janecek.
Cover design by Carolina Bucheli-Peñafiel.
Cover art by Erin Long.
Printing by Bookmobile.